# 12 Months of Encouragement

## Volume II:

## The Encourage Yourself Journal

### By: E. Brewster

**Copyright** © 2022

All Rights Reserved

**Publisher:** The Mason Publishing Company

*This Book contains privacy of the author you cannot copy or duplicate this book all rights reserved. No part of this publication may be reproduced, stored in a retrieval system, or transmitted in any form or by any means -electronic, mechanical, photocopy, recording, or any other- except for brief quotations in printed reviews, without the prior permission of the publisher. For information address Themasonpublishingcompany2020@gmail.com*

printed in the United States of America

**ISBN: 978-0-578-27630-4**

# *Table Of Contents*

Title Page

Copyright..................................................................1

Table Of Contents...................................................2

Acknowledgement..................................................4

Dedication...............................................................6

Introduction............................................................7

**Month 1** Rise........................................................8

**Month 2** Focused...............................................13

**Month 3** Determination....................................18

**Month 4** Peace..................................................24

**Month 5** Clarity.................................................29

**Month 6** Mindfulness.......................................34

**Month 7** Fearless.................................................40

**Month 8** Growth..................................................45

**Month 9** Grateful................................................50

**Month 10** Courageous......................................56

**Month 11** Limitless...........................................61

**Month 12** Destination......................................66

## *Acknowledgement*

This project is long overdue. It wouldn't have come to life without the support from my loving family and close friends. Thank you, Terrance, for always believing in me. You never let me give up and I'm so grateful for that. My kids, Michael and Allison, nephew and nieces, David, Jayla, and Kenedi, thank you for being my biggest fans. Momtie loves you. Mom and Dad, you're the best, I'm thankful I've always had your support. To my sister Munchie, thank you for looking over the journal and giving it your approval. It meant so much Big Sis. A special thank you to B. Rose for being the driving force behind me and this journal. You are God sent. Thank you to The Mason Publishing Company. You helped me make this dream come true. Nakendra, you are a gift, Thank You. To all those who have prayed for and supported me, thank you so much. I pray this journal inspires every person that touches it.

E. Brewster says Be Encouraged.

# *Dedication*

To my Owl Angel. You always supported me no matter what you were going through. You will forever be in the dedication section. Thank You J. I love you forever.

# *Introduction*

Sometimes you must encourage yourself to step out the tunnel. Keeping a journal; is a helpful way to keep you on track.

Let us begin…

I'm right here about to step out. The darkness is behind me. I must encourage myself to move forward. I can't step back. I must move forward. Here I go…

## *Month 1*

## *Rise*

I will rise above the ashes of all the things that burned me. I will Rise above the hurt that consumes my thoughts and ignites my fears. I will Rise above the guilt, shame, hurt, and defeat of my past. I will Rise above those that say I can't. I will Rise above procrastination. I will Rise above doubt. I will Rise above anything that keeps me from my purpose. I shall Rise.

# Word of the Month:

## *Rise*

Take a moment each day to journal about how you can rise above the daily obstacles thrown your way.

Date: / /

Date:  /  /

*Date: / /*

# *Month 2*

# *Focused*

I am walking in the fullness and Grace of GOD and your presence, (Fear, Doubt, Defeat, Drama, etc.) is not needed in this chapter of my life. I am Focused.

# Word of the Month:
## *Focused*

Take a moment each day to journal about how you can stay focused know matter what distractions you may encounter.

**Date: / /**

**Date:** / /

Date: / /

# Month 3

## Determination

The enemy can't stand my Faith...so he will use fear as a distraction to deter me from my blessings. I will not be moved.
I am Determined.
Three months down. Nine months to go. Let's Get It!

# Word of the Month:
## *Determination*

Take a moment each day to journal about your determination to achieve your goals.

*Date:* / /

Date:  / /

*Date:* / /

*You rose above your adversity. You remained focused and determined not to let fear distract you. You did it!*

*Three months down. Nine more to go. Let's Get It!*

*E. Brewster says Be Encouraged*

## *Month 4*
## *Peace*

I am here. I am thankful. I have been blessed with purpose and covered by Grace. I am flowing like a stream headed for greatness. I am calm. I am free. I am ready for my destiny. I am at Peace.

# Word of the Month:

## *Peace*

Take a moment each day to journal about how you can continue to keep your peace.

Date: / /

Date: / /

Date: / /

# *Month 5*
# *Clarity*

My vision is clear. I can see beyond the obstacles. I am focused. I have Clarity.

# Word of the Month:

## *Clarity*

Take a moment each day to journal about ways to keep clarity and remain focused.

Date: / /

*Date: / /*

Date: / /

# *Month 6*

# *Mindfulness*

I will be present. I will love and enjoy life. I will embrace each moment. I will cherish the right now. I will live. I will be Mindful.

# Word of the Month:
## *Mindfulness*

Take a moment each day to journal about the importance of mindfulness.

Date: / /

Date:  /  /

Date: / /

*You let Peace consume you. Your vision became visible with Clarity. You were Mindful to be present each day. You did it! Six months down. Six more to go. Let's Get It!*

*E. Brewster says Be Encouraged*

## *Month 7*

## *Fearless*

I will Accelerate my faith. I will Accelerate my actions. I will breathe and believe. I will not be afraid of where I am going because God is already there. I am Fearless.

## Word of the Month:
*Fearless*

Take a moment each day to journal about how to maintain your fearless Faith.

Date: / /

Date: / /

Date: / /

*Month 8*

*Growth*

I am blooming into my purpose. I am trusting the process. I am growing through what I go through. I am Growth.

# Word of the Month:
## *Growth*

Take a moment each day to journal about how far you have come and how much you have grown.

Date: / /

Date:  /  /

Date: / /

# Month 9

## *Grateful*

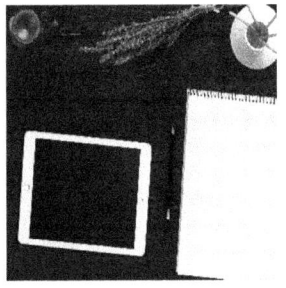

I will give thanks not just for everything
but in everything.
I am Grateful.

# Word of the Month:
## *Grateful*

Take a moment each day to journal about how grateful you are.

Date: / /

Date: / /

Date: / /

*You walked within your purpose with Fearless Faith. You chose to go through what you went through. You were grateful, not just for everything but in everything. You did it! Nine months down. Three months to go. Let's Get It!*

*E. Brewster says Be Encouraged*

# *Month 10*

## *Courageous*

I am strong. I am special. I am tough. I am loved. I am brave. I am determined. I am focused. I won't give up. I will push. I will remove my limits. I will look beyond my circumstance. I will stand on God's promises. I will fight. I will live. I shall be what God has called me to be. I will trust God. I am Courageous.

# Word of the Month:
## *Courageous*

Take a moment each day to journal about your courageous Faith.

*Date: / /*

Date: / /

Date: / /

# *Month 11*

# *Limitless*

My Faith in God supersedes what it looks like. I will not be moved by circumstance. I shall walk with purpose. I will speak with authority. I will take my victory by force. I

## Word of the Month:
*Limitless*

Take a moment each day to journal about how you are filled with limitless Faith.

Date: / /

Date: / /

Date: / /

# *Month 12*

## *Destination*

Faith over fear... One step at a time... Hope over doubt... One step at a time... Victory over defeat... One step at a time... I Am walking in Purpose. It is not always comfortable... But the final Destination is worth it.

# Word of the Month:
## *Destination*

Take a moment each day to journal about how you have overcome procrastination and made it to your destination.

Date: / /

Date: / /

Date: / /

*You were courageous despite your obstacles. You allowed your Faith to have no limits. You didn't let devastation determine your destination. Twelve months down. A lifetime to go.*

*You are more than a conqueror. You rose, stayed focused, remained determined, made your peace, found clarity, embraced mindfulness, showed up Fearless, grew through what you went through, remembered to be grateful, stayed courageous, worked with limitless Faith, and experienced the manifestation into your destination. I'm proud of you.*

*E. Brewster says Be Encouraged*

www.ingramcontent.com/pod-product-compliance
Lightning Source LLC
Chambersburg PA
CBHW050706160426
43194CB00010B/2018